EP

Creature Comparisons

Monkeys

Tracey Crawford

Heinemann Library
Chicago, Illinois

Customer Service   888–454–2279

Visit our website at www.heinemannlibrary.com

Photo research by Tracy Cummins, Heather Mauldin, and Ruth Blair
Designed by Jo Hinton-Malivoire
Printed and bound in China by South China Printing Company
10 09 08 07 06
10 9 8 7 6 5 4 3 2 1

Library of Congress Cataloging-in-Publication Data
Crawford, Tracey.
  Monkeys / Tracey Crawford.— 1st ed.
     p. cm. — (Creature comparisons)
  Includes bibliographical references and index.
  ISBN-13: 978-1-4034-8455-0 (hc) ISBN-10: 1-4034-8455-4 (hc)
  ISBN-13: 978-1-4034-8462-8 (pb) ISBN-10: 1-4034-8462-7 (pb)
  1. Monkeys—Juvenile literature. I. Title. II. Series.
  QL737.P9C73 2007
  599.8—dc22
                          2006007667

Acknowledgments
The author and publisher are grateful to the following for permission to reproduce copyright material: Corbis pp. **4** (bird, Arthur Morris), **5** (Frank Lukasseck/zefa), **10** (Gallo Images),**15** (Darrell Gulin), **18** (Philip Marazzi; Papilio), **19** (Keren Su), **20** (Tom Brakefield), **22** (Macaque monkeys, Yann Arthus-Bertrand); T. Falotico, ETHOCEBUS p. **22** (Capuchin monkey): Getty Images pp. **4** (fish), **6** (Michael Nichols), **9** (Peter Lillie), **11** (John Bracegirdle), **13** (Brian Kenney), **16** (Art Wolfe), **21** (Eastcott Momatiuk); Naturepl.com pp. **7** (Pete Oxford), **14** (XI ZHI NONG), **17**; Shutterstock p. **12** (Brian Tan); Carlton Ward p. **4** (snake, frog).

Cover photograph of a black howler monkey reproduced with permission of Nature Picture Library/Anup Shah and an emperor tamarin reproduced with permission of Corbis/Theo Allofs. Back cover photograph of a monkey in the rainforest reproduced with permission of Corbis/Philip Marazzi, Papilio.

Contents

There are many types of animals.

Monkeys are one type of animal.

All monkeys have fur.

All monkeys can climb.

backbone

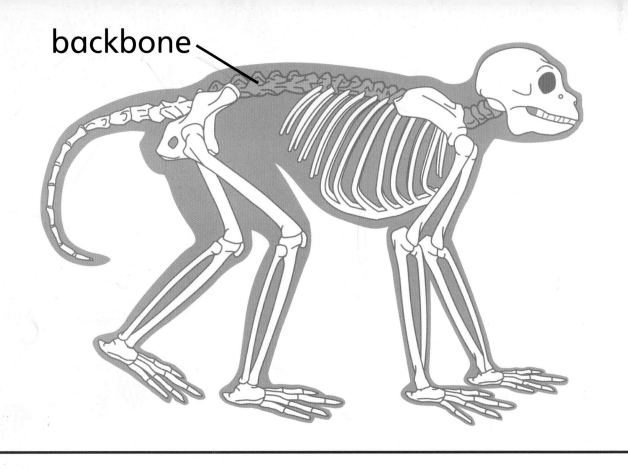

All monkeys have a backbone.

All baby monkeys get milk
from their mother.

Most monkeys have a tail.

But these monkeys do not.

Most monkeys have thumbs.

But this monkey does not.

Most monkeys live in trees.

But these monkeys do not.

Some monkeys are big.

Some monkeys are small.

Some monkeys live in warm places.

Some monkeys live in cold places.

Every monkey is different.

Every monkey is special.

Monkey Facts

These monkeys live where it is cold. They sit in warm water to keep warm.

Monkeys are very smart. This monkey uses a stone as a tool. It hammers a nut with a stone to open it.

Picture Glossary

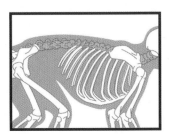

backbone the part of the skeleton that goes from the head to the tail

Index

Note to Parents and Teachers
In *Monkeys*, children are introduced to the diversity found within this animal group, as well as the characteristics that all monkeys share. The text has been carefully chosen with the advice of a literacy expert to enable beginning readers success while reading independently or with moderate support. Scientists were consulted to provide both interesting and accurate content.

By showing the importance of diversity within wildlife, *Monkeys* invites children to welcome diversity in their own lives. The book ends by stating that every monkey is a unique, special creature. Use this as a discussion point for how each person is also unique and special. You can support children's nonfiction literacy skills by helping them to use the table of contents, picture glossary, and index.